COLOUR THE PICTURES WITH CRAYONS OR COLOUR PENCILS AND FILL IN THE SPEECH BUBBLES!

COLOUR THE STORY!

LUCKY, IT'S DIWALI!

NALINI SORENSEN

ILLUSTRATED
by
SHAMIKA
CHAVES

HarperCollins*Children'sBooks*

To Lars,

Lucky? Actually, that's me. Because I have you.

- Nalini

First published in India in 2018 by HarperCollins Children's Books

An imprint of HarperCollins *Publishers*

HarperCollins Publishers India, Cyber City, Building 10-A, Gurugram, Haryana-122002, India

www.harpercollins.co.in

2 4 6 8 10 9 7 5 3 1

P-ISBN: 978-93-5302-351-5

Typeset in Helvetica Neue Regular, 14pt/ 20

by Shamika Chaves, Mumbai, India

Printed and bound at MicroPrints India, New Delhi

MIX
Paper
FSC FSC™ C218906

This product is made of FSC®-certified and other controlled material.

HarperCollins Publishers, Macken House, 39/40 Mayor Street Upper, Dublin 1, D01 C9W8, Ireland

1
Boom! Pow! Boom! Frzzzzzzz!

Boom! Keeeeuuuu … BOOM!
Frzzzzzzz! Boom!

I run from one room to another, tail between my legs. 'Woof! Woof! Woof!' I bark at the window. What is going on? Are things falling down? Is Adit playing with a ball inside the house again? What's going on? It is all so LOUD!

Boom! Frzzzzzzzz! Boom! Pow! Keeeeuuuu … BOOM!

I run as fast as I can and try to jump on the bed, and bury my head under the pillow.

'Oh, poor thing, Mummy!' says Adit, although he himself jumps, every time he hears these sounds. I move towards him, to show him I understand, but he turns away from me. He actually tries to avoid me as much as possible.

'Come here, Lucky! Come!' says Zara, with a smile on her face, bending down and slapping her thigh.

BOOM
FRZZZZZ
POW

But before I can move, Mummy comes over and carries me in her arms. I feel safe and slip my nose in her curved elbow. She kisses me on the top of my head and says, 'Don't be scared, Lucky. They are just firecrackers. It's Diwali … a festival we celebrate once a year. It will pass soon enough.'

'Poor girl! It all sounds so much louder in her ears,' says Zara.

'What are you talking about now?' asks Adit, jumping violently with the next round of firecrackers.

Boom! Boom! Frzzzzzz!

'Woof! Woof! Woof!'

'Oh my GOD. You don't listen to a word I say. I'm glad I'm going to become a vet, when I grow older, and not you. Dogs hear at a different frequency than us. And they can hear with each ear independently. Everything sounds much louder in her ears. If you weren't such a doofus, you'd have figured it out already. Lucky has been with us for five months, and if you'd just spend some time with her, you'd notice stuff. The funny thing is, you both seem to have this in common. You both jump at the sound of firecrackers! Maybe you can bond over that,' replies Zara.

'Mummy, did you hear that?' whines Adit. 'She totally, TOTALLY just called me a doofus, right in front of you.'

'Are you both bickering AGAIN? These Diwali holidays will feel even longer for me, if all you two do is fight, fight, fight! Zara, there's no need to be rude to your brother. Go and do something else. Read a book! Just stop picking on him like a pesky elder sister. Adit, you don't become a doofus because someone calls you one. And …'

Boom! Boom! Boom! Frzzzzzz!

'Woof! Woof! Woof!'

'Oh, Lucky!' Mummy says, holding me close.

'It's quite clear who the favourite child in this house is,' snaps Zara.

Mummy smiles. 'Well, to be fair to Lucky, I don't hear her calling anyone names!'

Zara leaves the room, but not before tickling me on my neck, and kissing my head. She really does love me. I can feel it. Adit also leaves the room, but doesn't come anywhere near me. Mummy sits on the rocking chair, cuddling me in her arms. I feel safe and snuggle in closer.

2

Lucky, That's ME!

I was born in another home, not in this one. I had five other brothers and sisters, who all looked just like me. Long ears, black-and-white patches in varying combinations. We were a litter of Cocker Spaniel puppies.

I can still remember us all squealing and pushing each other to drink milk from my mumma. I can't remember everything, but I can remember us wrestling with each other a lot.

umma would push her snout
/een us and separate us, and
n give us a big lick. Sometimes the
k was gentle, and sometimes it was
ot so gentle. Sometimes we got a
nibble too, depending on what we
were doing.

The days all squished together
with us all squished together,
doing pretty much the same thing.
And then suddenly one day, there
were people who came into our room
to see us.

And just as suddenly, we were
one less.

'Where did they take her, Mumma?'

I whimpered. And I got a gentle lick. 'They've adopted her. She is going to their home to take care of them now. You too will soon go to your new home. And you too will take care of your new family.'

'What? I don't want to go! I want to stay here!' I cried, snuggling closer to her.

For the next few days, I jumped every time I heard footsteps walking into the room. But my mumma was right. From six, we were five, then four, then three.

And then, there was *that* day. I remember it so clearly. I was sleeping in my favourite spot, under the bed, near its leg, when my mumma gently pushed me with her snout and said, 'Come, you must come and see this new family.' I sleepily rolled out, along with my brother and sister, and found four pairs of eyes staring at us.

It was a mummy, a daddy, a boy and a girl. The boy just peeked at us and screamed and ran out of the room. The mummy said, 'See? This is exactly why we need a puppy. He can't continue being like this. Once we have a puppy at home, he will stop being afraid and grow to love our pet. Pets teach kids so many things. It's good to have a pet.'

The girl sat right down on the ground and took all three of us in her lap.

‘Can’t we take them all?’ she begged, rubbing my fat belly.

‘No,’ said the daddy firmly. But his kind face spoke otherwise.

My sister and brother walked away from the girl after some time. But I stuck around, just because it was nice feeling her fingers tickle my belly. I moved my back leg up and down, as it REALLY tickled me, and she laughed. ‘I think, Mummy, this one has chosen us.’

The daddy looked at the mummy with a small smile on his face, and gave a tiny nod. The mummy bent down and patted my head. She picked me up from the girl’s lap, nuzzled my head and said,

'What do you know? I think so too.'

And that's how I reached their home. As soon as we walked in, I ran around in circles, sniffing at all the things in the room. 'Isn't she adorable, Zara?' asked the mummy. I looked up and saw the girl nodding her head vigorously. Ah! The girl was called Zara.

Everything in their home was so interesting and so very different. All the smells were new, the sounds were new, and the light seemed brighter. I was excitedly checking it all out. Zara, the mummy and the daddy watched me with pure joy. But the boy sat on a big chair with his feet curled up.

He didn't seem quite so joyous. He simply looked intently at my every move. 'Why don't you pat her, Adit?' the daddy gently asked. I turned my head to them, and wagged my tail. 'No way!' he hurriedly replied. Ah! The boy's name was Adit.

And right on cue, Zara said, 'We need a name for her! How about Cindy? She looks like a Cindy to me.'

'There's nothing Cindy-like about her,' replied the mummy. 'I think we are lucky …' And I jumped on the mummy's knees, wagging my tail and barking.

'AHHHH! Lucky?' asked my new mummy, her eyebrows raised high and

LUCKY

a huge smile on her face. I cocked my head to one side, looked at her, wagged my tail and barked, 'Woof! Woof! Woof!'

'That's it! She's Lucky! And we are so lucky to have her!' said Mummy.

And everybody laughed. And that's how I got my name.

Everyone, except for Adit, started calling me to them, 'Lucky, come! Lucky, here!' It was all so much fun! I was so excited that I bent down and did a little wee.

And suddenly, they weren't laughing anymore.

'Take her out!'

'Put her on the grass!'

'Bring the mop!'

'Eeeewwwwww!' (This was from Adit.)

I've been living here for five months now. I don't wee or poop in the house anymore. But it took a few months with Adit, Zara, Mummy and Daddy screaming all these things every time I did go in the house. I really don't know what the fuss was about.

I now only chew their shoes when I'm bored and if they have left me alone at home. I think they deserve that. Don't you?

3
The Party Prep

'I can't wait for my pool party! I can't WAIT! I'm going to be eight! EIGHT! EIGHT! That's two short of double digits! The big one-oh!' says Adit happily, stretching his arms out on either side. 'I just love the water, and it's still so hot. There's nothing better than splashing in a pool when the weather is like this!' he continues.

'I agree, Adit. A pool party was a great

BIRTHDAY
BOY!

idea. But we will need to go to the pool early and decorate. I've got everything ready — balloons, streamers, party pops, ribbons,' says Mummy. 'And I can't believe you are turning eight either! Such a big boy!'

'Everyone is really excited, Mummy. Samir said he couldn't wait, and Chris said he had new swim goggles that he was bringing. And …'

'Thank God you said I could have a friend too, Mummy. I can't imagine hanging out with a bunch of eight-year-old kids,' grumbles Zara.

Boom! Boom! Keeeeuuuu … BOOM! Frzzzzzzz! Boom!

'Woof! Woof! Woof!'

I jump up and run straight to Mummy. Adit drops his spoon. It hits the floor with a loud clatter.

'It's all right, Lucky. It's just the Diwali firecrackers again, my girl,' Mummy coos right in my ear. I stuff my nose under her elbow.

'You act like you are so big. You are just twelve yourself,' Adit growls at Zara.

I can see he is getting upset with Zara. I jump off Mummy's lap and run over to him to lick his toes and comfort him. He immediately moves his feet up on the chair. I sniff his knee, wag my tail and go to Zara. Adit wipes his knee. Zara pats my head, bends over to kiss my head and tickles my belly.

Boom! Boom! Frzzzzzzz!

'Woof! Woof! Woof!'

I jump up and whine loudly. Adit shakes too. Zara rolls her eyes at him and picks me up.

'Oh, you poor thing,' she whispers in my ears. 'I'll tell you a secret. It looks pretty at night, but I'm not big on firecrackers either. Don't tell anyone, okay? And especially don't tell *him*.'

I give her two huge licks on her

nose and eyes, and she squeals with pleasure.

Zara puts me back down, and I run off to find my squeaky toy, or a sock to shake and chew. Daddy's socks are normally lying around and are nice and chewy.

'Come, help me get everything in one place, Adit, so we have it ready for tomorrow. I have told the pool uncle that we will go there two hours early to decorate,' says Mummy.

Adit and Mummy carry the bags and boxes with the decorations and line them by the front door.

I go there and sniff around, and he

immediately says, 'Mummy! She's going to chew them all. Remember what she did to my shoes? I loved those shoes!'

'Uh-uh-uh,' says Mummy firmly to me. 'No touch, Lucky!'

'Should we keep it all up on the table instead?' Adit asks.

'I think it's okay. She can't chew any of this,' says Mummy. Then she takes one look at my happy, smiling face and says, 'Ermmm ... famous last words? Okay. Let's move it to the table, Adit. Just to be safe.'

4
Rangoli

Buzzz-buzzz! Buzzz-buzzz!

It is the doorbell. I love when it rings. It means someone has come to our home!

I run to it and bark and bark. 'Woof! Woof! Woof!'

'Shusshhh, Lucky,' says Zara. And then, 'Oh hi, Chris! Come on in!'

'Hi, Zara. Is Adit home?' asks Chris.

'Yes, he's in his room …'

'LUCKY!' yells Chris.

I adore Chris! He is the nicest, smelliest boy. We have a whole routine going. First I jump on him, then he has to bend, so that I can put my paws on his shoulders and pull him down. And THEN, he lies down on the ground and lets me lick his face and nibble his nose. I remind him, 'Woof! Woof! Woof!'

'Okay, okay, Lucky! Let's do this,' says Chris. And we go through our routine. It's the best feeling ever. Chris loves it and I love it. He screams with delight as I lick his face and nibble his nose.

'Chris!' says Adit. 'Eeewwwww! How do you even let her do that to you!'

'It's our thing. I love it. There is nothing like dog kisses,' says Chris, with the hugest ever smile on his face. 'It makes everything all right again.'

'As I said – Eeewwwww! Do you want to wash your face?' asks Adit.

'Nope. I'm okay. I can't believe you've never let her do this to you. It's the best,' Chris replies, grinning from ear to ear.

Chris is Adit's best friend and quite conveniently lives right next door to him. The two boys are in and out of each other's homes all day.

I trot behind Chris, hoping to sleep at his feet, but Adit quickly closes the door to his room. Ah! Too bad! I was too slow! I stay on guard outside. You never know if something were to happen. I like taking care of my boys. It's the best thing about being a dog.

As I close my eyes, Mummy walks by. 'You want a walk, Lucky?' This is the best moment of my day. I run around and between Mummy's legs. I jump on her. I can't sit still for even a second. My tail has a life of its own and wags and wags. 'Woof! Woof! Woof!'

'Calm down, Lucky. You are going to trip me! Let me fasten your leash. Lucky!' says Mummy sternly, though I can hear the laughter in her voice.

She finally gets the leash on me, and off we go. As we step out of the door and start walking towards the stairs, Mummy meets Chris' mum. She loves me too. So I jump on her and give her a warm welcome and a couple of kisses.

The two of them start talking, and something new catches my eye. I see something on the floor in front of Chris' front door. I set off to explore. It's some sort of powder. I sniff it. It has a faint smell, but nothing I can place. I put my paw on it, and it moves around. I rub my paws in it in circles, around and around. I rub my head in it and start to lick it, when I hear Mummy say, 'LUCKY! Oh no! Karina, she's destroyed the rangoli outside your door!'

Karina laughs loudly. ‘It’s okay. Lucky, you look lovely in pink and green! Perfect on your black-and-white fur!’

Boom! Boom! Keeeeuuuu … BOOM! Frzzzzzzz! Boom!

I drop my head, my tail goes down, and I run back home. It’s just so loud!

5
Balloons POP!

Mummy, Daddy, Zara, Adit and I are at the pool. Zara's friend, Isha, is also here. She is helping Mummy, Daddy and Zara with the decorations.

Daddy is pumping up the balloons. Mummy is tying them up. And Isha and Zara are stringing them together.

'Just so you know, I'm pumping them faster than you are tying them,' Daddy teases Mummy.

'That is not true and you know it!' Mummy replies.

Zara says, 'And you think Adit and I squabble. Seriously?' She rolls her eyes at Isha.

'This isn't a real squabble, Zara,' says Isha.

Daddy says, 'Better stop the chitter-chatter you two, or we will start commenting on how slowly you are stringing them together.' All four of them laugh.

Adit and Chris are already in the pool, and I am running from the balloon-blowing people to the boys in the pool. I feel tiny drops of water fall on me from the boys splashing in the pool. It feels nice, but I don't go in the pool. I've never really been comfortable around this pool. It's the smell. It just doesn't smell very nice. I see some pool water on the floor, and I lick it up. Uggggh! It does not taste nice! Uggggh! It is such bad tasting water!

I run back to the balloon-blowing people and try to grab one of the balloons. It's like a giant ball. I'm sure I can chew on it. And ... BANG! I nearly jump out of my skin! Now I get it! It's a firecracker! Is it in the balloon? Why are they calling it a balloon if it is a firecracker? Goodness! That was loud!

BANG

I yelp loudly and quickly run away, with my tail between my legs, back to the boys in the pool! There might be bad tasting water there, but at least it is not loud!

Zara and Isha run after me. Zara carries me and says, 'Oh, Lucky! You are silly, and a little unlucky! Don't go after the balloons. Balloons pop and go boom! Oh, you poor thing!'

She holds me close, and I can feel myself calming down. My heart stops racing, and I start to feel like myself again.

This human world is really strange. And often quite loud.

6
The Party

There are so many children here, and I am just so happy. They have patted me, scratched me behind my ears, tickled me, chased me – and I love it all.

I'm a bit tired, but I gamely go on. I'll grab a nap later.

There is LOTS of food around, and the smells are all terrific. I twitch my nose and move to the table with the food. Something smells so yummy up there.

'Uh-uh-uh!' Mummy says to me. 'Not there, Lucky!'

My ears flop down apologetically, and I go to her. Yes, I'm not supposed to be there. I know the rules. But I just can't help myself.

I am keeping well away from the balloons, and I am sticking to the part near the pool, with all the children.

Daddy is playing a game with the children. It's a lot like 'Fetch'. He is throwing something in that bad tasting water, and then the children are all

HAPPY BIRTHDAY
ADIT

screaming and scrambling and splashing about and getting it back to him.

Chris splashes some water on me. I take a step backwards.

'Does she swim, Adit?' Chris asks.

'I don't know,' Adit replies. 'She's never been in. It's a pool rule that dogs can't go in.'

'Kids! Time to eat! Come out and eat! You can go back in to play after, but everything is warm and ready now,' Mummy calls out.

All the children start to make their way out in a slow procession, with towels wrapped around them. Adit and Chris are last; they are sitting by the pool and waiting for the others to go first.

Chris stands up and says, 'I need to go to the toilet, Adit. I'll be back in two.'

7
What Just Happened?

As Chris walks away, there is a flurry of activity near the dining table. Adit looks at me, turns his back to me and then looks to the table where the food is placed. I think he is starting to feel hungry. I am too!

Boom! Keeeeuuuu … BOOM!
Frzzzzzzz! Boom!

'Woof! Woof! Woo …'

I jump. I try to run away. It's so very loud.

My paws slip on the water on the ground, as I scramble around in panic, and suddenly, I lose my grip. I slip, and I'm in the pool with a huge splash.

I feel myself going down, down, down.

I kick my legs about. I can hear the water splashing. I am so scared. I try to open my mouth to bark, and that awful tasting water fills my mouth! What just happened? Help! Why is no one helping me?

Adit hears the firecrackers and jumps just a little too. He hears something splash behind him, and doesn't bother looking. But then, after a few seconds, he turns around slowly, looking confused.

He sees me, in the pool, struggling.

'Lucky! Oh my God! Mummy! Daddy! LUCKY!' and without any hesitation, he jumps into the pool and swims fast towards me. He grabs me below my tummy and pulls me up. It's in the shallow end of the pool, and his feet can touch the ground. He stands up, quickly, carrying me out of the water. It's the first time he's ever carried me.

Mummy, Daddy, Zara, and everyone else at the party turn and watch the entire scene unfold in horror. It seems like they are all frozen, and then they all run towards us together. A little like someone pressed pause, and then pressed play again.

Suddenly there are many, many pairs of hands around us — holding us, carrying us, helping us out of the pool. Mummy grabs me out of Adit's hands. 'Are you okay, Lucky?' I blow my nose loudly. And shake my head fast from side to side. Ah! I can hear properly again.

'What just happened?' 'What just happened?' everyone is asking.

'It was the firecrackers! You know how she runs when she hears them.

She fell in the pool, trying to run away from the loud sounds,' Adit replies.

I get out of Mummy's hands and shake myself vigorously; drops of water are flying everywhere – just as they do after my bath. I actually feel completely okay now. Mummy is trying to rub me down with a towel. I am trying to escape from her.

'You are such a little hero!' Daddy says to Adit. 'You know how Diwali is essentially about bringing light where there is darkness? You did just that for Lucky today, Adit. You brought light!'

Adit turns to look at me. I look back at him. I run to him and try to put my paw on him. Daddy is right! I'm trying to tell him that. He is about to push me away, as he usually does, I can feel it … but … something stops him. Something is different. He slowly bends down. I let out a happy little bark and lick him very gently on his face. I'm so, so happy and want to jump on him too, but I don't want him to pull away.

Adit closes his eyes in horror and starts to pull away. Then, much to my surprise, he squeals in delight.

SILLY ZARA
MY SWEET LUCKY FELL IN THE POOL

ADIT &
LUCKY
2018
THE BEST BIRTHDAY PARTY
EVER. I LOVE YOU SO MUCH LUCKY.

‘It’s so tickly and so soft!’ he laughs.

‘Lie down on the ground, Adit,’ Chris yells. ‘It’s the best!’

Adit slowly lies down on the ground, and lets me lick him all over his face and nibble his nose, just as I always do to Chris.

He laughs and laughs and moves his head up and says, ‘It IS the best, Chris.’

Boom! Keeeeuuuu … BOOM!
Frzzzzzzz! Boom!

And Adit forgot to jump, and I forgot to bark.

ABOUT THE AUTHOR

Nalini Sorensen is an award-winning children's author, who loves spending time with children and looking at the world through the wonder of their eyes. She believes that life is too short to not laugh, and seems to always attract highly humorous situations in her real life. She lives in Mumbai, with her husband, two sons and dog. There is a lot of love, a lot of laugher and a lot always going on in their home. Nalini's other books include *While You Are Sleeping, Papa's Marathon, Dada's Useless Present, The Star that Saved the Day, Number March* and *Alphabet Dress-Up.*

ABOUT THE ILLUSTRATOR

Shamika Chaves is an illustrator and graphic designer based in Mumbai, India. Born into a family of artists, she successfully pursued a degree in applied art and best expresses herself through her illustrations. She enjoys the freedom of hand-rendered illustrations, often using digital media to enhance them. Her work is inspired by the simple joys of everyday life. She lives and works in her cosy little home with her husband, Christopher, and her five-year-old tortoise, Sebastian. Shamika's first book, *Your Journal of Memories*, is being published by HarperCollins India. Visit @shamikasdoodles on Instagram or shamikasdoodles.com to learn more about her work.